Black Cats and White Wedding Dresses

Folk Customs

North American Folklore for Youth

Black Cats and White Wedding Dresses

Folk Customs

Thomas Arkham

Mason Crest

Mason Crest
370 Reed Road
Broomall, Pennsylvania 19008
www.masoncrest.com

Printed and bound in the United States of America.

First printing
9 8 7 6 5 4 3 2 1

Library of Congress Cataloging-in-Publication Data

Arkham, Thomas.
  Black cats and white wedding dresses : folk customs / Thomas Arkham.
      p. cm.
  Includes bibliographical references and index.
   ISBN 978-1-4222-2491-5 (hard cover : alk. paper) — ISBN 978-1-4222-2486-1 (hardcover series) — ISBN 978-1-4222-9256-3 (ebook)

  1. Folklore. 2. Superstition. 3. Manners and customs. I. Title.
  GR72.A75 2012
  398.2—dc23
                                    2011022555

Produced by Harding House Publishing Services, Inc.
www.hardinghousepages.com
Cover design by Torque Advertising + Design.

Contents

✳ Introduction

by Dr. Alan Jabbour

What do a story, a joke, a fiddle tune, a quilt, a dance, a game of jacks, a holiday celebration, and a Halloween costume have in common? Not much, at first glance. But they're all part of the stuff we call "folklore."

The word "folklore" means the ways of thinking and acting that are learned and passed along by ordinary people. Folklore goes from grandparents to parents to children—and on to *their* children. It may be passed along in words, like the urban legend we hear from friends who promise us that it *really* happened to someone they know. Or it may be tunes or dance steps we pick up on the block where we live. It could be the quilt our aunt made. Much of the time we learn folklore without even knowing where or how we learned it.

Folklore is not something that's far away or long ago. It's something we use and enjoy every day! It is often ordinary—

and yet at the same time, it makes life seem very special. Folklore is the culture we share with others in our homes, our neighborhoods, and our places of worship. It helps tell us who we are.

Our first sense of who we are comes from our families. Family folklore—like eating certain meals together or prayers or songs—gives us a sense of belonging. But as we grow older we learn to belong to other groups as well. Maybe your family is Irish. Or maybe you live in a Hispanic neighborhood in New York City. Or you might live in the country in the middle of Iowa. Maybe you're a Catholic—or a Muslim—or you're Jewish. Each one of these groups to which you belong will have it's own folklore. A certain dance step may be African American. A story may have come from Germany. A hymn may be Protestant. A recipe may have been handed down by your Italian grandmother. All this folklore helps the people who belong to a certain group feel connected to each other.

Folklore can make each group special, different from all the others. But at the same time folklore is one of the best ways we can get to know to each other. We can learn about Vietnamese immigrants by eating Vietnamese foods. We can understand newcomers from Somalia by enjoying their music and dance. Stories, songs, and artwork move from group to group. And everyone is the richer!

Folklore isn't something you usually learn in school. Somebody, somewhere, taught you that jump-rope rhyme you know—but you probably can't remember *who* taught you. You definitely didn't learn it in a schoolbook, though! You can study folklore and learn about it—that's what you are doing now in this book!—but folklore normally is something that just gets passed along from person to person.

This series of books explores the many kinds folklore you can find across the North American continent. As you read, you'll learn something about yourself—and you'll learn about your neighbors as well!

Life is full of many, many people and things. Somehow, our brains find a way to find patterns and make sense out of everything.

ONE
Building Patterns

Words to Understand

coincidence: A coincidence is when two things happen at the same time for no real reason.

folk: Folk has to do with ordinary people.

customs: Customs are practices that groups of people follow. They do the same thing the same way, year after year.

superstitions: Superstitions are beliefs that people have that aren't backed up by science or facts.

traditions: Traditions are ways of thinking and acting that are passed along from parents to their children for many years.

hypothesis: A hypothesis is an explanation for why things work a certain way. Scientists use hypotheses as a starting point for finding out more. They use experiments and other ways of studying the world to find out if their hypotheses are true or false.

Life is full of so many things. School, family, friendships. Homework and chores, the Internet and television. Boys and girls, grownups and children. Happiness and sadness, anger and laughter. It can get confusing!

But the human brain tries to make sense out of it all. It tries to find patterns that happen again and again. When our brains find those patterns, we feel like we can control our lives a little better. We know what to expect next.

Your brain has been making sense of your world ever since you were first born. Words are one of the things that help you see patterns in the things around you. When you were learning to talk, you learned the names for lots of different things. At first, maybe you thought all furry things were kitties. Then you learned more names for furry things—doggie and bunny and horsey. Now, you're probably learning even more words for animals, like mammal, rodent, cattle, and felines. You've probably never thought about it, but all these words help you make sense out of the world.

When you were younger, you also learned a lot of rules about the way life works. Things you take for granted now were what you were busy learning back then. You worked hard to find rules that would help you know what was going to come next every day. For example, you learned that it got dark at night when you went to bed. Then after a while, you understood that days are measured this way. Every time you go to bed, it's the end of the day. Every time you get up in the morning, it's a new day. Once you understood this, you could grasp words like "tomorrow," "yesterday," and "today."

For little people who take naps every day, though, this can be more confusing than you might think! Some preschoolers who take long naps in the middle of the day think the morning is one day, the afternoon another. Eventually, they learn that it's sleep AND darkness that make a new day. It takes a while to find the right patterns to make sense out of life.

Children are not the only ones who look for patterns like this. Grownups do too. Just like children, adults feel more comfortable if they can tell what's likely to happen next. They look for rules that will make sense out of life's mix of happiness and sadness.

And sometimes, just like preschoolers who get mixed up about naptime, people make mistakes. They come up with a rule they think is true—like black cats bring bad luck or Friday the 13th is an unlucky day—but the rule is based on *coincidence*. Something bad happened a few times someone saw a black cat or on a Friday that happened to fall on the 13th of the month. People decided then that the black cat CAUSED the bad thing. Or the bad thing happened BECAUSE it was Friday the 13th. They didn't realize it was just coincidence.

These rules and patterns often become *folk customs*. They may be *superstitions*, things people believe. They may be *traditions*, certain ways people always act. They all serve a purpose. They give people a path to follow when life gets confusing. They help people make sense out of things that happen.

People who spend time together—whether in a family, in an area of the world, or in a religion—often share these customs. They pass them along within the group. They hand them down to their children. Then their children hand them on to THEIR children.

Some people think that everyone who believes superstitions is silly or stupid. You may think you're too smart to believe a broken mirror causes 7 years of bad luck. You know better than to think that a black cat is unlucky! But remember, the people who came

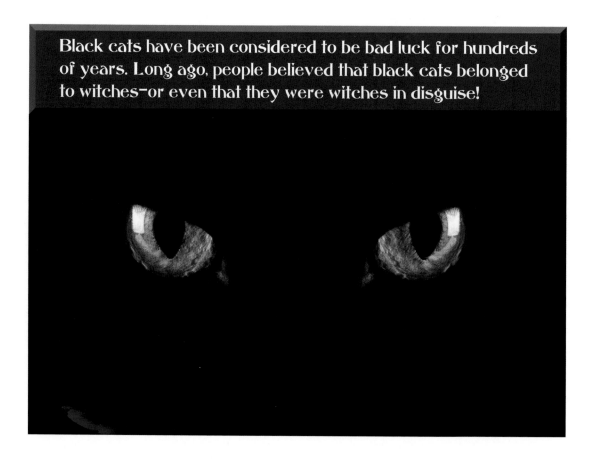

Black cats have been considered to be bad luck for hundreds of years. Long ago, people believed that black cats belonged to witches—or even that they were witches in disguise!

up with these ideas were just doing their best to understand why things happen the way they do. In a way, they were like scientists.

Scientists watch to see the way things happen. They do experiments, so that they can watch the same thing over and over. Then they make a **hypothesis**, a guess that explains why things happen the way they do. Sometimes they're right. Sometimes they're wrong. But they won't know they're wrong until they gather more information.

That's also the way people create customs and superstitions! They're the beliefs that people have built up over time. They built them around things they have seen happen. For them, these beliefs made sense.

Today, we may have more information. We know that black cats don't cause bad things to happen. We know that we'll never find a pot of gold at the end of a rainbow. And stepping on a crack in the sidewalk isn't going to break our mother's back!

But other superstitions still seem to make sense to us, even today. Maybe we don't completely believe them. But we believe them a LITTLE. For example, a lot of people really do feel a little worried on Friday the 13th. And if you find a four-leafed clover, you probably feel lucky.

And we still follow many of the same customs our ancestors did. We may not even think about why we do things the way do. It just seems like the RIGHT way to do things. For example,

Have you ever wondered why we put candles on a birthday cake? The custom began in ancient Greece, where a cake was given to the Moon Goddess. Candles were put on the cake to make it glow like the moon—and then people blew out the candles and made a wish. Thousands of years later, we're still blowing out candles!

brides almost always wear a white wedding dress. And birthday cakes usually have candles burning on them—and when you blow them out, you make a wish.

Folk traditions and customs give our lives a pattern. They make us feel more comfortable in the middle of all the things that happen in our confusing world. And sometimes, they're just plain fun!

DID YOU KNOW?

Wedding dresses weren't always white. In fact back in the 1700s, a bride might wear any color to her wedding. An old poem went like this:

Married in grey, you will go far away.
Married in white, you will have chosen all right.
Married in black, you will wish yourself back.
Married in red, you'll wish yourself dead.
Married in blue, you will always be true.
Married in pearl, you'll live in a whirl.
Married in green, ashamed to be seen.
Married in yellow, ashamed of the fellow.
Married in brown, you'll live out of town.
Married in pink, your spirits will sink.

In those days, most women couldn't afford to buy a new dress to wear only one day. A bride's dress was often her "best dress," whatever color that might be. It wasn't until later in the 1800s, when dresses could be bought ready-made, that women began to wear white dresses just once on their wedding days. At first, the white dress meant that brides had never loved anyone besides their husbands. Today, it's just tradition!

It's fun to try to see into the future—but a little scary too.

✳ TWO
What's Going to Happen Next?

Most people are a little scared of the unknown. They like to feel they understand what's going on. They want to know how things work. When they don't, they feel frightened.

So it's no wonder we sometimes feel like the future is scary. We don't really know what's going to happen tomorrow—or next year. We don't know what to expect. What lies ahead might be wonderful—or it could be terrible. Either way, we wish we KNEW. Then we could plan ahead.

Lots of people would say they don't believe in fortunetellers. But those same people probably still read their **horoscopes** in the paper. Or they kind of believe some of the superstitions that predict what the future holds. These beliefs make the future seem a little less frightening. They help people feel they have a better idea what to expect.

Different groups across North America have different beliefs about the future. They all have something in common, though. They all think that everyday events can tell us what will happen next.

Pennsylvania Dutch Fortunetellers

The Pennsylvania Dutch aren't really Dutch—but they do live in Pennsylvania. They're a group of people who came from Germany and Switzerland more than 400 years ago. They settled in what is now the state of Pennsylvania.

Many of their **descendents** still live there today. Most of these modern-day Pennsylvania Dutch probably don't believe all their ancestors' superstitions. But they still repeat them.

Here are some of their sayings:

> A picture falling from the wall means someone in the family will die.

The designs formed on water that freezes on Christmas Eve are
   omens for the future.

If you sweep on Good Friday, you will have many flies all
   summer.

Omens from the Ozarks

The Ozarks are another region of North America. Parts of
Missouri, Arkansas, Kansas, and Oklahoma lie within the
Ozark Hills. Settlers came to the area early in the 1800s. Living
together there, they came up with their own superstitions
about the future. Today, their great-grandchildren and great-
great-grandchildren still repeat some of these sayings:

   If you spill salt at the table, your family will get in a big fight with
      each other. The only way to end it is to pour water on the salt.

   If two people use the same towel at the same time, they will be
      sure to have a fight. If by accident two people take the same
      towel to dry their hands, they quickly twist it between them.
      That's said to "take the cuss off it."

   If two friends are talking as they walk along and they walk around a
      tree, one on each side, they will have a serious quarrel soon.

   When you visit someone, if you meet a flock of geese you can
      know you are a welcome guest. If you run into pigs on the
      road, though, your host will wish you would go away.

New England Predictions

New England is in the northeastern corner of the United States. People there have always eaten a lot of fish. That's why they have a lot of superstitions there about fish, boats, and fishermen.

A salty line down the center of the fish was called the "dream line." If you weren't married and you ate a dream line before going to bed, your future wife or husband would come to you in a dream.

If you watch a ship out of sight, you will never see it again.

Sunday sail, never fail.

Friday sail, ill luck and gale. *(This means it's good luck to sail on Sundays, but bad luck to sail on Fridays.)*

Other North American Superstitions About the Future

Across North America, people have all sorts of ways of predicting the future. Even something as common as an itchy nose can have meaning if you're looking for signs about the future! Here are some examples:

If your nose itches, if your nose itches,
Somebody coming with a hole in his britches.
(This means you're likely to have a poor visitor.)

If you have an itchy nose, you're going to kiss a fool.

If your nose itches on the right side, a boy or man is going to visit you.

If your nose itches on the left side, a girl or woman is coming to see you.

Itchy eyes, ears, and hands can also have meaning. If your right eye itches, get ready for bad luck. An itchy left eye, though, means good news is on its way. If your ears itch or burn, someone is talking about you. When your right ear itches, someone is saying good things about you. But an itchy

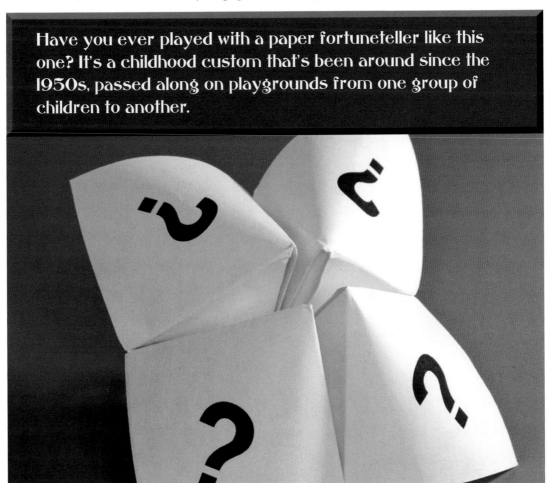

Have you ever played with a paper fortuneteller like this one? It's a childhood custom that's been around since the 1950s, passed along on playgrounds from one group of children to another.

left ear means that somewhere someone is saying something bad about you. If your left hand suddenly begins to itch, you'll soon receive a present you weren't expecting.

Sneezing also helps people predict the future. If a woman sneezes before breakfast, she can expect company before noon. If she sneezes during breakfast, however, she knows that two or more people will leave her home before sundown. And if she sneezes with food in her mouth, she will hear of a death sometime in the next 24 hours.

This rhyme spells out other sneezy superstitions:

Sneeze on Monday, sneeze for danger.
Sneeze on Tuesday, kiss a stranger.
Sneeze on Wednesday, sneeze for a letter.
Sneeze on Thursday, sneeze for something better.
Sneeze on Friday, sneeze for sorrow.
Sneeze on Saturday, see a friend tomorrow.
Sneeze on Sunday, the Devil will be with you all week.

The world is full of other omens that tell the future. Even something as ordinary as a mole on your skin can help you peek into the future.

Mole on the neck,
Money by the peck.

Dreams are another way to look into the future. For thousands of years, all around the world, people have been paying attention to their dreams. Here are some of the sayings about dreams:

To dream of muddy water means trouble lies ahead.

To dream of snakes means you'll have a fight with an enemy.

A dream about a white horse means that sickness or death will come to your family.

If you dream of death at night, a wedding is on its way. But if you fall asleep in the daytime and dream of death, expect disaster.

If you dream of pigeons or doves, a you're about to fall happily in love.

The first dream you have in a new house will always come true.

Across North America, people love to try to look into the future. Even if they're just pretending, it's still fun. That's why they read the horoscope section in the newspaper. They crack open Chinese fortune cookies. They look for good omens in the palms of their hands. Children love to play with toys like 8-Balls and paper fortunetellers.

We can't really know what the future holds—but it's fun to try!

People have no control over the weather. But that doesn't stop them from trying to find ways to make sense out of it.

✳ THREE
Making Sense Out of the Weather

Grownups love to talk about the weather. For your great-great-grandparents, the weather was even more important than it is today. The weather wasn't just something to talk about back then. The weather shaped people's lives. If weather was good, crops grew well. People had plenty of food and money. If the weather was bad, they might go hungry. Entire towns could become poor.

Many superstitions and customs grew up around the weather. We may think they were silly. But today scientists still study the weather. They try to make sense out of what's going to happen. Will it be hot or cold this week? Will it rain or will the sun shine? Is a blizzard on its way? Will a tornado touch down? Weather is still important to people's lives. It shapes what we can do tomorrow. It changes our plans.

That's why people report what's going to happen in the weather on television, the radio, and the Internet. These reports are based on science. But they're still not always right! The weather often takes us by surprise.

Lots of times, weather folklore seems to make almost as much sense as what the Weather Station has to offer! Different groups across North America have come up with different ways to understand the weather.

Ozark Farmers' Weather Folklore

People who live in the Ozarks today have television and the Internet, just like the rest of the world. They're not separated from the rest of the world the way their ancestors were. The old ways of thinking and acting are no longer as strong.

But many farmers still live in the Ozarks. They take the weather very seriously. They need to be able to tell when rain and snow and ice are on their way. Bad storms can mean disaster for

Weather is very important to farmers. Too much rain can destroy crops—and so can too little.

a farmer. So they take into account the sayings their fathers and grandfathers passed on to them. They know that their **predictions** aren't always right. But neither is the weather report on the news!

The Ozarks are filled with hills and hollows. This means that weather conditions can be different across a short distance. If your prediction doesn't come true in the sky over your head, it might still be right a mile or two down the road!

Here are some of the common weather sayings in the hills of the Ozarks:

If rabbits play in a dusty road, it will rain.

If a dog eats grass, it will rain.

If a cat sneezes, it will rain.

If a pig carries a piece of wood in its mouth, a storm is on its way.

When horses' tails look fluffy, a **drought** will soon be broken. (**Static electricity** *could make the horses' tails fluffy. And static electricity can be caused by a thunderstorm that's on its way.*)

If cattle and horses refuse to drink during dry weather, expect a cloudburst.

If a cat yawns and stretches, expect good weather.

When fat from the cream in a cup of coffee collects at the edge of the cup, rain is coming. If it collects in the center, dry weather is ahead.

For every 100-degree day in July, there will be a 20-below day in January.

Some Ozark weather signs are so common that they have been turned into folk sayings like these:

If a cock crows when he goes to bed,
He'll get up with a wet head.

When the morning sun is red,
The ewe and the lamb go wet to bed.

Rain before seven,
Shine before eleven.

A sunny shower
Won't last an hour.

A bushel of dust in March
Is worth a bushel of silver in September.

Onion skin mighty thin,
Easy winter coming in.

According to Ozark folklore, certain days of the week or year are particularly important when predicting the weather. For instance:

If it rains on Monday, it will rain every day that week.

Friday is always either the "fairest" or the "foulest" day of the week.

If the sun "sets clear" on Tuesday, it will rain before Friday.

The sun shines every Wednesday, if only for a moment. If by chance, however, the sun does not shine on Wednesday, expect violent weather, maybe even a tornado.

When rain falls on the first Sunday of the month, expect rain the following three Sundays.

If it rains on Easter Sunday, the following seven Sundays will also be rainy.

The last Friday and Saturday of each month rule the weather for the month to come.

If July 2 is rainy, the summer will be moist, and crops will grow well. If July 2 is dry, there will be drought for six weeks.

If November 11 is cold, expect a short, mild winter.

The weather on December 25 is connected to the rainfall and temperature of the following summer. A mild Christmas means a heavy harvest. (Unfortunately, a "green Christmas" is also said to bring a "fat graveyard.")

The first 12 days of January rule the rest of the year. The weather on January 1, will be the weather for the rest of the month. The weather on January 2, will be February's weather. January 3's weather will be March's weather, and so on.

Weather signs can be helpful and provide a sense of control—but some old Ozark farmers went a step further. They made weather charms. Burning brush along a creek was thought to bring rain. Hanging dead snakes belly up on fences did the same. A farmer might also try to "charm up" rain by pouring water in the middle of a dusty field. Plowing a field was also said to bring rain.

Pennsylvania Dutch

The Pennsylvania Dutch have their own set of weather signs. Some of these are much like the weather signs used in the Ozarks. The Pennsylvania Dutch, however, were a very religious community. Their spiritual beliefs sometimes show up in their weather omens.

The cry of the whippoorwill is a sign of rain.

If chickens lose their feathers in August, the coming winter will be severe. If they lose their feathers in October, the winter will be mild.

When people got desperate after a long stretch of dry weather, rainmakers often tried various strange things to try to bring rain. The men here believed that these funnels would pull down the water from the sky.

If the lower legs of chickens are well covered with feathers, the winter will be severe.

If it is clear on the Visitation of the Virgin (July 2), there will be no rain for six weeks.

The weather for the year can be determined on Christmas night by taking 12 onions, naming them each for a month of the year, hollowing them out, and then filling them with salt. The onions in which the salt melts will indicate the wet months of the year.

DID YOU KNOW?

People in the Ozarks sometimes got desperate if dry weather lasted too long. When that happened, they might ask a rainmaker's help. A rainmaker was someone who could bring rain. Old newspapers tell stories about rainmakers. For example, in 1929, the owner of a canned tomato company offered $50 to anyone who could bring enough rain to save the tomato crop. In a 1946 newspaper, a woman told about a rainmaker who used the Bible. He knelt down on the ground. He bowed three times toward the east. Then he repeated the sixth verse of Psalm 72—"He shall come like rain upon the mown grass, as showers that water the earth." According to the newspapers, in both these cases the rainmaker brought rain.

Rain on Whitsunday (Pentecost—the seventh Sunday after Easter) will be followed by seven rainy Sundays.

If it rains on Good Friday, look for high winds and little hay.

When you see many women out on the street, expect rain the following day.

When you see spider webs on the lawn, expect rain.

New England Weather Signs

The weather was just as important to New England fishermen as it was to Ozark and Pennsylvania Dutch farmers. A storm at sea could bring disaster or even death. Good weather, though, meant good fishing. New Englanders watched the weather carefully. They collected their own set of signs for predicting the weather.

> When the donkey begins to bray,
> We surely shall have rain that day.

Gulls fly inland before a storm. They fly out to sea when a stretch of good weather is on its way.

Bats flitting about late in the evening mean a good day tomorrow.

Water birds will scream before a storm.

Butterflies appear early in the spring when fine weather will follow.

If cornhusks stick to the ear and do not pull off easily, the winter to come will be stormy.

When the oysters bed deep, the winter will be hard.

If a chicken's gizzard comes away easily from the inner skin, expect an "open winter" (with little ice or snow).

If you find a school of herring in January, put away your overcoat for the year.

Weather Superstitions
from the Rest of North America

Other regions of North America have their own weather *lore*.
The farmers of Texas predict rain whenever. . .

a herd of cattle settle on the side of a hill.

a quail whistles after sundown.

a tree frog hollers.

ants close the holes in their mounds.

a rainbow appears in the morning.

a silver maple shows the back sides of its leaves.

cats lick their feet.

Texans expect snow when. . .

the smoke from a chimney goes to the ground.

a pig squeals in the winter.

wild hogs begin to make beds in the creek bottom.

And Texans count on clear weather whenever. . .

a rooster crows after a shower.

locusts are heard.

if larks fly high and sing for a long time.

You and your family may have your own weather folklore. Have you ever heard that if you wash and wax your car, it's sure to rain? Or have you looked at wooly bear caterpillars to predict whether the winter ahead will be long or short?

These beliefs and customs make the world seem less mysterious and scary. They give people a sense of power and confidence. Through stories, sayings, and customs, weather lore (like all folklore) helps make life a little easier to manage.

If Punxsutawney Phil sees his shadow we can expect another six weeks of winter!

GROUNDHOG FOLKLORE

Across North America, one of the most well-known weather signs is Groundhog's Day. On February 2, the groundhog is supposed to come out of his hole to look around. If the sun is shining and he sees his shadow, he will go back to sleep. That means there will be six more weeks of winter weather. If the sky is cloudy, and he cannot see his shadow, he will stay awake. This means spring is just around the corner!

Groundhog's Day started out in Europe. People there thought of February 2 as the beginning of the growing season. They called the day Candlemas. In France, it's a bear that comes out of its cave to look for its shadow on the 2nd of February. In Germany, it's a badger. The groundhog superstitions are a good example of the way folklore travels from country to country. When it does, it often changes a little bit.

According to modern North American folklore, the "official" groundhog is Phil. Phil lives in Punxsutawney, Pennsylvania. Every February 2, newscasters go to Punxsutawney to report whether Phil sees his shadow or not. You may have even seen a movie about this event called *Groundhog's Day*.

If you find a four-leafed clover, do you feel lucky? If you do, you're experiencing an ancient folk belief that's been around for at least 500 years.

FOUR
Luck

> **Words to Understand**
>
> *far-fetched:* Something that is far-fetched isn't very believable. It doesn't seem to be based on facts.

No matter how hard we try, we can never really control EVERYTHING about life. Superstitious people can never know what will happen tomorrow. Neither can scientists! Life will always take us by surprise.

"Luck" is the word we use for these surprises. Anything we don't really understand about life gets lumped under good luck or bad luck. Even people who believe God controls our lives often believe in luck. Even scientists believe in luck, at least a little bit! In fact, most of us believe in it.

Luck can't really be understood. But many folk beliefs try to predict ways to bring good luck. Folk customs are also meant to help us stay away from bad luck. Some of them may seem *far-fetched* or silly. Some of them we may take for granted. We may follow these customs and never think about why we do what we're doing.

Sometimes these customs are different in different parts of North America. Sometimes they're very much the same. Either way, for hundreds, maybe thousands of years, these customs have helped people feel a little more in control of life.

Signs of Bad Luck from Ontario

Eating any fruit found growing in a graveyard brings bad luck.

If you leave a knife on the table when you go to bed, you will have bad luck.

Cutting your fingernails on Sunday brings bad luck.

Stepping over a grave is bad luck.

Watching the moon go down is unlucky.

Singing or whistling in bed will attract bad luck.

Ozark Beliefs About Luck

It is bad luck to take a saltshaker directly from a person's hand. The correct thing to do is to wait until the other person sets the shaker on the table and withdraws her hand. Then you are free to pick it up without causing bad luck to either of you.

It is bad luck to lend or borrow salt. If you must borrow salt, never return it. Instead, pay back an equal amount of sugar, molasses, or some other household good.

Omens from Nova Scotia

Upon setting out on a trip, if you meet a redheaded woman, turn back or you will have bad luck.

If a woman is your first guest on New Year's day, you will have bad luck. If a man is your first guest, however, your luck will be good.

If a squirrel runs across your path, it means good luck.

If you see the moon over your left shoulder, it means bad luck

If you see it over your right shoulder, it means good luck.

Some omens for good and bad luck are common across many parts of North America—like these:

Never give a knife as a gift. Knives must always be paid for, even with a penny. That's the only way to avoid bad luck for both the giver and the receiver.

See a pin, pick it up,

All day long you'll have good luck.

See a pin, leave it lay,

Have bad luck all through the day.

It is bad luck to put on your left shoe before your right.

Lifelong good luck comes from finding your initials in a spider web.

Black cats are signs of bad luck.

Walking under a ladder will bring bad luck.

Breaking a mirror brings 7 years of bad luck.

Bad luck comes in threes. (If something bad has happened, expect
  two more bad things to happen before your luck changes.)

Opening an umbrella inside brings bad luck.

"Good luck," we say to someone getting married or starting
a new job. "Wish me luck," we tell our friends as we set off to

A ladybug, a horseshoe, and a four-leafed clover all
mean the same thing: good luck!

do something new. "I'm sorry you've had such bad luck," we tell someone who has had a lot of bad things happen to him. "This is my lucky day!" we cry when something good comes our way. Signs and omens make us feel as though we can tell what's going to happen next. Like other customs, traditions, and superstitions, they help us feel more at home in a world that's sometimes scary. They help us live with all the things we'll never understand. They give us hope. Sometimes they even make us laugh!

DID YOU KNOW?

Some insects are thought to bring good luck:

crickets

daddy longlegs

ladybugs

Find Out More

Folk Customs Around the World

www2.geog.okstate.edu/users/lightfoot/folk.html

Lucky Charms

www.halloween-website.com/superstitions.htm

Silly Superstitions

www.islandnet.com/~luree/silly.html

Weather Folklore

www.weatherwizkids.com/weather-folklore.htm

Picture Credits

Fotolia
    Aamon: pg. 44
    Connelly, H.D.: pg. 26
    Dusk: pg. 14
    Maldesowhat: pg. 29
    Oily: pg. 10
    Saloutos, Pete: pg. 18
    Schweltzer, Elena: 16
Nebraska State Archives: pg. 32
Wikimedia Commons: pg. 23

Index

About the Author and the Consultant

Thomas Arkham has enjoyed reading folklore since he was very young. He has worked as a public school teacher for many years, and is now starting a new career as an author.

Dr. Alan Jabbour is a folklorist who served as the founding director of the American Folklife Center at the Library of Congress from 1976 to 1999. Previously, he began the grant-giving program in folk arts at the National Endowment for the Arts (1974-76). A native of Jacksonville, Florida, he was trained at the University of Miami (B.A.) and Duke University (M.A., Ph.D.). A violinist from childhood on, he documented old-time fiddling in the Upper South in the 1960s and 1970s. A specialist in instrumental folk music, he is known as a fiddler himself, an art he acquired directly from elderly fiddlers in North Carolina, Virginia, and West Virginia. He has taught folklore and folk music at UCLA and the University of Maryland and has published widely in the field.